GITTENS
THOUGHTS
FROM WITHIN

A Collection of Poems by
Daughter and Father, Debbie and Lionel Gittens

by

Debbie V. Gittens-Hans

DORRANCE
PUBLISHING CO
EST. 1920
PITTSBURGH, PENNSYLVANIA 15238

Dorrance Publishing Co
585 Alpha Drive
Pittsburgh, PA 15238
Visit our website at *www.dorrancebookstore.com*

ISBN: 978-1-6376-4363-1
eISBN: 978-1-6376-4647-2

This Book is dedicated to...
These poems were inspired by my inner thoughts of life and family.

I dedicate this book to my children Jessica Leeann Goode and my son LT. Darius G Gittens. I love you both with each fiber of my being. Never stop reaching for the ocean/stars. My granddaughters Amari and Averi you both bring me so much joy. I love you both very much from now to the end of my time. Whatever your passion is in life, fulfill it to your best. To my husband Henry Hans Jr. for encouraging me to get my work published. To the writer and poet Lionel J Gittens, my dad Rest In Peace, for in reading your work I was inspired to publish our work, and to my friends Michelle and Javanese that have given me the support and love throughout the years.

To my spiritual prayer worrier Maureen, though, you have moved on to our heavenly home. I have to say, thanks for all the prayers and guidance throughout the years that kept me afloat. Rest in Peace my dear friend.

I give God the Glory and Praise for in both my darkness and joyful moments; He touched my inner thoughts, which allowed me to express my life experiences through my writings.

Impatient With the Lord

Day 1
My Lord, this is it
Today I surrender all of me to you
Show me; teach me to do your will
I give my all to you.

Day 2
My Lord, this is really it.
No turning around
I am yours forever.
I give my all to you.

Day 3
My Lord, haven't you heard me?
I said, "This is it"
I belong to you now
What do you want me to do?
I give my all to you.

Day 4
My Lord, I'm losing patience with you.
I have been trying to talk to you
To let you know I'm ready to surrender
My life to you
I give my all to you

Day 5
My Lord, what is the problem?
You said, "Rely on you"
Trust in you, depend on you.
I'm trying to do these things
But you are not paying attention
I'm willing to truly give my all to you

Day 6
My Lord, I'm going crazy
I can't go on like this
What is my purpose on earth?
I'm about to fall again
I'm willing to give my all to you

Day 7
"My child, your purpose on earth
is to be patient with me and love one another
It took me six days to create the universe
 and now you want me to
fix You in one day.
You are so impatient.
like I said in the beginning
'Trust me and you will be okay'
You must be patient with me as
I am patient with you
and know that I am Lord
the answer to all things"

Why Wait For Tomorrow

Why wait for tomorrow
Tomorrow may never come
Why wait for tomorrow
When you can do good things now
Why wait for tomorrow
Because it's today that counts
Why wait for tomorrow
When someone needs you right now
For tomorrow may never come

Love today, for tomorrow may never come
then you wouldn't have to say
why did I wait for tomorrow
when tomorrow may never come

Show your love today
For tomorrow may never come
Show your love to someone today
For tomorrow may never come.
Then you wouldn't have to say,
I didn't have to wait for tomorrow
because tomorrow may never come

As the Tears Flow

She sits and sits hoping for some relief
But the tears flow and flow
She prays and prays hoping for relief
But the tears flow and flow
When would the tears stop flowing?
The refrigerator does not work
The washing machine does not work
There is a gas leak
And no work to be found
As the tears flow and flow
When would the tears stop flowing?
When would there be some relief?
As the tears flow and flow

Pray

Pray, Pray, Pray
That is all they ever say
Pray, Pray, Pray
And everything will be all okay
There is no food
There is no place to shelter
But they say
Pray, Pray, Pray
There is no love
But they say Pray, street walker, homelessness
Life has fallen apart
but they say Pray
There is nothing left but death
But they say Pray, Pray, and Pray
When these prayers would be answered
Aren't we all children of...?

Strength Within

Though your eyes may fill with tears
and no one may understand your pain
I do recognize the hurt in them
I do recognize that you may feel alone
in your sadness it's okay to cry
It's okay to feel sad
and it may seem the tears will never stop
but remember this, there is only one
who can ease the pain, dry the tears
and take away your sadness
That one is you
You are strong and all strength is within you
 So cry, be sad, and feel the loneliness today
In the end these things will all go away because
You are strong to get rid of them
So say to yourself
Get up and get out, for I am strong and all
Strength is within me.

Untitled

The sky is my rooftop
The trees my blanket
The ocean my floating bed
Laughter heals my soul
and affection lifts my spirits
If you love the earth
Fly with me
Into dreams of the unknown

You

You are sweet, you are so sweet
Sweet as the ripe fruit juices
running down my hands
You touch me and it feels magical
It reaches my whole being
From my head to my toes

Oh, how I love your touch
It's soft and gentle like
Cotton balls against my skin
Your breath on my face is
like the warm summer wind

A Wish

If wishes can come through
I will wish you here
Lying next to me, holding me close to your beating heart
If wishes can come through
I will wish for your lips to be pressed against mine right now
If wishes can come through
I will wish that we can sit in a room filled with golden balloons, holding
each other, listening to love songs
If wishes can come through
I will wish that your heart and mine can be one

As I await your return,
I just wish that in this room
It's just you and me and the raindrops on the windowpane
It's just you and me in the forest with the birds singing in the early morning sun
It's just you and me in the garden of flowers and fruits
It's just you and me on the earth full of love and peace
I wish that I can hold on for you and believe my wishes will come through
Oh, my love, if wishes can come through

Chance

Chances are you will make it
Chances are you will not make it
But if by chance you do make it
Remember I was there
But if by chance you don't make it
Still remember I was there
 For I was there when you needed a chance
A chance to show love
A chance to follow your dreams
A chance to ask for forgiveness
I gave you a chance
For by me giving you a chance
I hoped your life would be a litter easier
So give someone a chance and
Then you will be able to say
"I was there when you needed a chance"

Plans

Everyone makes plans
no matter who they are.
Simple plans or major plans
Plans to work or not
Plans to cook, clean, or not
Plans to have a vacation or stay at home
No matter where one is in life
Plans are always being made
One is happy when plans come through
One is sad when plans do not come through
No matter where one is in life
Plans are always being made
But if they come through or not
No plan lasts forever
because death conquers all plans
 In the end, plans never last

Sacrifice

I sacrificed my life for you
You my parents
You my friends
You my husbands
You my children
Everything that I did was for you

When I was growing up
I tried to be what you my parents
wanted me to be
To live the life you wanted me to live
I sacrificed my thoughts for you
because I wanted to be
what you wanted me to be
and my friends,
I wanted to please you
I sacrificed myself for you
I listened to you and did as you wanted

You, my husbands
I put away my dreams so you all
Could pursue your dreams
You, my children
I sacrificed everything for you
because you didn't ask to be in this world
I sacrificed my being for all of you
because I loved you so much
True love is about sacrifice
and if that was my purpose
to sacrifice my life for you
Then so be it
because I believe
Love is a sacrifice.

How Will I Remember Her

How will I begin to remember her?
I hear her voice saying "Let's pray,"
I hear her voice saying
"You know who to take your disappointments too."
I hear her voice saying,
"He is the answer to all your needs."

How will I begin to remember her?
I see her smiling face because she answered His call.
I see her smiling face because she obeyed by reaching out to others.
Her hands, her feet, and her heart He gave to her to do His work on earth.
And so she did with a humble and loving heart.
She never said no. She did not know how to say no.
She always answered His call.

How will I begin to remember her?
She saying yes to help all He sent her way.
She smiled and reached out to all
those who needed help, a listening ear,
some comforting words, even some financial help.
She was His obedient servant.

Oh, how will I remember her?
I have shed many tears, and she comforted me with the Lord's words of
love and understanding.
My heart is filled with joy because you weren't just a friend;
you were like a big sister, an angel to me.

How will I remember her?
I will always remember her saying,
"It's not my will Lord but your will be done."

I'll remember her telling me "Always do his will."

I'll remember her as a silent worker doing the Lord's work and not looking for recognition.

I'll remember the love she showed me.

RIP

My Sister and I

When I first knew you, you were a baby
I used to love to tickle your feet
Just to see you pull your feet and toes back
Just to hear you laugh
then you were gone

When I first knew you as a toddler
You were taken away from me
Oh, how I cried for you
and cried, and cried
Oh, how I missed you
I felt all alone

When I first knew you in elementary school
I loved to pass by your home to play with you
I missed going and picking governor plums with you.
Oh, how I wanted to live with you
Oh, how I missed you
Then I was gone, gone to another country

When I first knew you as a teenager
I was in another country
We wrote sometimes, but it was not the same
I was sad and happy at the same time
I was sad because I thought I would never see you again.
I missed you. I missed not being able to come and see you and just talk
about nothing special.
I was happy because I would not be sad anymore
of not being able to live with you.

When I first knew you as an adult
 I saw you after all those years
I thought you were so beautiful.

I just knew that we would be together now

We were together, but it was not the same
I felt alone, though we had good times
It was not the same. For what I was looking for was not there.
At times I felt the love was one sided.

Oh, how I cried and cried wishing I had my sister.
Life felt all alone again.
for you are here but not with me.
Now I'm left to imagine.
What it would be like to grow old with you.

Forgive Me

Oh, my Lord, forgive me for going astray
Oh, my Lord, I thank you for dying on the cross for me
Oh, my Lord, I thank you for taking away my iniquities
Oh, my Lord, today I commit to follow you
And if by chance I stumble and fall into sin
I ask you, Lord, to touch me with your everlasting love and forgive me
so I may return my soul to you.

Lord, I Praise You Because...

Oh, God, my love and protector
I'll give you praise today because...

Oh, God, my love and healer
I thank you because...

Oh, God, my love and strength
without you I'm weak

Oh, God, my love and king
I'll worship you because...
I'll spread your news because...

Oh, God, my love and forgiver
I'll say praises to you each day
I'll do your work because...........
I'll lift you up to all because........
I'll lift you up to all

Friendship

Dedicated to Michelle

You bring happiness
Your friendship has stood the test of time
Most of all, you are her best friend
A friend that she will never give up
A friend who loves her just the way she is
A friend who tells her when she wrong or right.
A friend that values her opinion
A loyal friend you are.

She felt sadness when you weren't around.
Oh yes, she was miserable when you weren't around.
Then you came to the rescue.

You sacrificed your comfort for her and her children.
When she needed a place to stay, you were there to offer yours.
You gave up your personal space.
You gave up your bedroom so they could be comfortable.
You never thought once about yourself.
And there are so many other beautiful attributes about you.
You were always there for her.

The world should learn from you what unconditional love is.
You are all about caring and helping a friend
Not just caring and helping but giving of your whole self, unselfishly.
She shed tears of joy because of the love you gave to her and her children.
Never had she ever felt so special
She thanks her God for sending her an angel like you.
Her life would be empty without you

She valued your friendship
You are true friend.
She never wants for anything

If your generosity were to be measured
It would be wider than the ocean
taller than the mountain range and as big as the universe.
Your kindness can't be compared, and it is priceless.
No other human has ever given up themselves like that to her.
You are truly amazing individual.
That is what true friendship is about,
 the unselfishness of the giver never asking for anything in return.

You are an angel.
You gave unconditionally, never wanting anything in return.
The world needs more angels like you.

Friends are flowers that never fade
A loyal friend is a gift from God
Life has no Blesssing greater than a true friend

Mother

Oh, mother, how I long for your touch
How I long to hear you say I'm sorry
How I long to hear you say I love you
But these words never came

Oh, mother, why you gave me away?
Oh, mother, where were you when I needed you?
How I long to know you
How long must I cry for you?

Oh, mother, my life seemed empty
Oh, mother, I needed you
How long I dreamt that we would have a
 special mother-daughter relationship.
How long must I feel abandoned?

Oh, mother, time is passing by
And you have yet to embrace me

Oh mother, when will you ever show me love?
How long must I wait?
How long before I hear you say I'm sorry?
How long before I hear you say I love you?
But these words never came.
RIP

A Broken Shoe of Love

Oh the Sun
How beautiful you shine?
As I journey to my spiritual moment
It Happened...
It Broke...
Oh No!... Oh No!...
I must Go!... I must Go!...
my spiritual journey halted
I rushed to my car
Raced to my dwelling place
retrieved another
Raced back to my spiritual journey
There he stood!...
There I stood!...
because of a Broken Shoe
A new beginning of Love, for the two
because of a Broken Shoe

Early Morning Sun

It is early in the morning; there is no movement of leaves except the morning waking the pine needles at the very top of the beautiful tall pine trees. A slight wind moves through the branches at the top, swaying it back and forth. The pine needles are swaying, enjoying the rise of the early morning sunlight.

Big trees, small trees, fat trees, skinny trees, old trees, young trees, even small bushes trying to see the sun. The sun peeps through the branches and casts its sunlight upon the leaves. There are so many trees, long branches and short branches all unique in their own way. Some trees are straight, and some are bent. The happiest trees are the ones straight because they receive the beautiful early morning sun way at the top. The tiny trees and small bushes are trying very hard to push their way up for a little bit of the warm morning sunlight. Those that are bent are bending towards the sunlight trying to get that early morning sunrise. All shapes of trees, branches, and leaves all hoping to get a little bit of nature's beautiful sunlight.

The morning has truly coming alive, for the trees and animals are ready to play. The trees of the forest are the animal's playground. All creatures are coming alive because of the early morning sunrise.

The male crickets are making the early morning chirping sound by rubbing their wings together. "Wake up" is what is being said. "The sun has risen."

A spider forms a web from one tree to another and then again from one branch to another. The early morning sun gleams through the web as a lady spider walks across her web bridge while carrying her sack of babies on her back as she enjoys the morning sun.

The squirrels awaken and begin to play tag between the trees and branches. As one jumps from branch to branch while the other one chases. Up and down the trees they go from branch to branch as the new day begins. As the early morning sun arrives.

Vines climb up the trees reaching for the early morning sun. As they climb, they squeeze and choke the trees, forcing themselves up to the top for the early morning sun. Everything must survive by the early morning sun. As the vines squirm like snakes up the trees, the trees begin to take on different shapes. At times, a tree may look as if it is shaping itself into a person's head, or it may look like it has arms and a body. All because of the reaching vines. The bending of the branches as the vines push themselves around and around, across and across, changing the shapes of the branches in the early morning sun.

The beautiful evergreen, which may be used for a Christmas tree, looks like a monster in the woods.

Peck, peck as the woodpecker makes its sounds in the early morning sun. He pecks on his tree to let the rest of the trees know he is awake and he must begin his music while the birds of the air began to sing as they sit on the tree tops in the early morning sun. Nature is beautiful in the early morning sun.

Omega
Dedicated to Roland, Irene, and Verna

Absolute darkness
A transformation within;
Relative to time and space
Luminous celestial crate
A Creation of the Grand

Suddenly a mutable impact
Removing all that's intact
As before, darkness comes once more.
After many eons, another impact
Deducting what's intact, as all went.

Emerging, the hydro-thermo-vent
With iron, sulfur, and a catalysis in the interior,
Tis the building block of the earliest bacteria
In this primordial soup, the gift began

With life beneath and in time above,
The Creator's work was near completion
With satisfaction and consideration,
The time had come for his image on the land

There is a negative, and a positive
There is a north and south
Therefore, man should have his spouse
Now with all creation here,
The time had come to make adoration clear.
From so many past eons,
We give thanks, for this millennium

Nature's Beauty

Sparkling stars in the sky
A sliver moon just floating by
Against the background of a dark night
Nature's beauty gives a wonderful sight

Nature's riches give sparkle and shine
For your pleasure and for mine
There is no beauty that can replace
Neither far nor distance place

The formation of birds going to
the night rest
It can be classes to be the best
The parent body of young birds
Travel far and wide
To get substance to be satisfied

The moon divides itself in quarters
And the oceans do the same
For nature always takes the blame
When things don't turn out for gain
Without the moon, darkness there be right
Such darkness, that is called the night

My Lonely Heart

Oh, how my days have lengthened
into weeks.
and the weeks stretched into months
as my heart is sad and sore
however, I wish to see you once more

Though nothing aids this yearning heart
or touches my innermost fear.
for I do recall the many months and years
how we held our love
from day to day.

I sit here, sad, now and groan
with my life all on my own
An apprehension that you would be
with me once more.
As I incessantly gazed at the door

I would take you gently by the hand
And hold you, as I did before
However, my dear, I know
This longing can never take place
For, unfortunately, my dear, sometime ago
We have placed you in your resting space.

I Love You

"I love you" is a special phrase
When used by true lovers, cannot be erased
When used by philanderer
Leaves broken hearts forever

It becomes a form of deception
With meaningless feeling when spoken
"I love you"
Is as sweet as the nectar in a flower
Such a phrase, will be echoed forever

Though this phrase is common
When I speak these words to you
It's deep and precious
From my soul, it must be true

My mind is void
I thought of nothing new
But, when I saw you,
To see your smiling face
Made my heart begin to race

"I love you"
Words from the beginning of time
With feelings that're sublime
Will be heard
From many, many more
That's coming behind

My Soul Partner

I have been looking for my twin soul
Though I found you, and lost you
Now, I know we are far apart
My eyes do weep such bitter tears
For moments lost, I cannot bear

My love, you were too quick for me
My mind and head grew cold
I could not see you
But we will meet again
At another time and place

And when again, our path do cross
Once more, my twin soul,
I hope fate will hold
I have learned well this time
Next time I will not need another sign

For I shall recognize you at a glance
And our lives should be a wonderful dance
Because forever we shall be together
And nothing else will matter

If

If I could walk beside you
If I could hold your hand
We'd walk along together
Then you would understand

If love could last forever
If dreams could be made true
They would safely be in my heart
And I'd share them with you

If my wishes could come true
And you said "Yes, I do"
I would be in paradise
And so also would be you

If I could talk to you
And tell you how I feel
If you could give me that chance
Then and only then
I would be enhanced

If I had my way
We would be together day after day
So that you could say
If this is happiness, let it stay

If you listen for a moment or two
I would get the chance to say
How much I think of you

If;
If,
If.

Trinbago

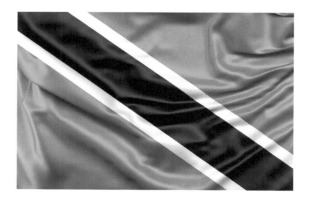

I reminisce of days gone by
When all "ah we"
See the yellow leaves of the mortel tree
The kaskadoo, the roti, the rice and peas
In which we were always pleased

The rice and peas with salt-kind
Represents its carnival time
To see the "Moko-jumbie, the Jab Jab"
"Cane and Abel"
As we jump up till we dead

At Easter weekend
The Kaskadoo is "boss"
With vegetable, greens and tomato we toss

The legend could be true
For I am always yearning for you

The roti, parata, and dalpuri
represent the celebrants of Duwali

Which is liked by all "ah we"
And, to hear such as
"by the way" Gimae a "bus-up dae"

Trinidad, an island of plural society,
Can be example to many
The Negro with their Carnival
The Indian with their Duwali
The Chinese with their Double Ten Day
We all share without a bother

From North to South
With all the rumbles
Don't leave out the Indian "DOUBLES"

Boyhood

Dedicated to my brother

Standing on a plateau of this tropical paradise,
I recall of days with my little brother standing by my side
"Which way?" he asked.
"Throw a leaf in the air," I replied
He smiled with delight

No matter where I travel
Or where on earth I roam
There is a place in Trinidad
That is forever home

I enjoyed watching the ripples in a clear cool stream.
The sunshine pierces the water,
making rock fishes and pebbles gleam.
Onward the water goes through a perpetual motion
as it heads in the direction of the ocean,
passing villages full of people on a mission.
Pity, they take no time to listen
but if they could, would they understand?
The stream's important task at hand

Such memories
The jewel in my crown
For the hills
We went up and down
Yet that was yesterday
With me such will stay.

The Family Tree

Down the branches of ancestral line
A search to take one back in time
Asking questions from aunts and uncles
Who knew more of the tree
Whilst we sat and dined
To understand the family line

Pictures were brought out
This was your Mother's sister
And from another, I saw
My grandfather's brother
Old letters of years gone by was another
Showing what my father's brother acquired.

With fading notes and prints
We explore by gone age
Turning every leaf, reading every page
It's amazing what the old ones did
As some had reacted with much rage

From my experience
I would say
"Don't delve too deep into the family tree"
There were some things that astonished me
Wishing I had from such depth, flee

As I learned my cousin Martha
as named after my father's mother
My sister Mary,
was given the name of her great aunt
Obviously, this lingered on my memory
What all this could be

The Wind

The rains had arrived
To give its blessings on the crops
As the docks had opened for the ships
Both farmers and stevedores became conscious of rewards

The spirit of fulfillment was here, for a short while;
There would be harvest for home and abroad thus
The farmers and the stevedores would have their fill

Such desires and forecasting was short lived
The rains increased and so were the winds that accompanied
 A sense of fear arose

The birds had departed
This increased wind and rain and to date
had given them an indication;
that the joy in one's breath
had turned to sorrow
Leaving nothing worthwhile for tomorrow

The crops destroyed, the habor likewise
Denying home and abroad

The Apology

To apologize for an error
Is no disgrace
It's better to keep a friend
Than lose a face

We are not perfect
And, at some time will err
Therefore don't hesitate
Eat the bitter cake

A friendship is precious
Such will last to the end
For it's a gift from the Gods
And it crosses all boundaries

As the wind is playing
In the branches of the tree
A message of love rustling
For friends as you and me

It's better to apologize than
to go with a sad face

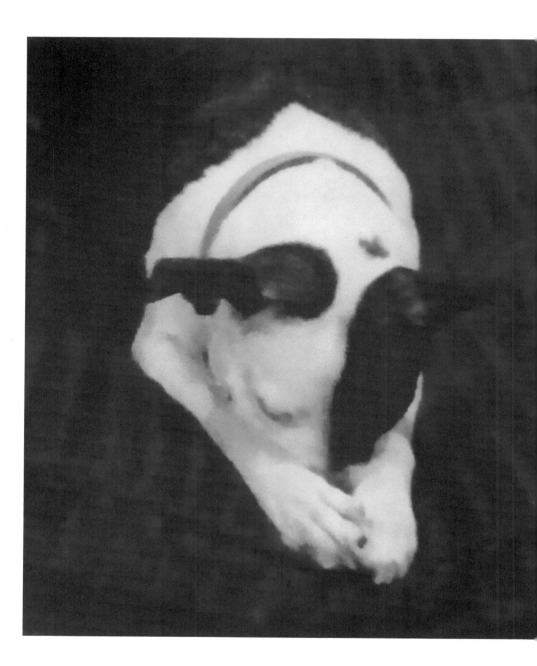

"Don't do wrong to others"

"It's better to forgive than to bear hate"

"Forgiveness is a virtue; try it sometimes"

"Practice forgiveness; it strengthens you"

"Love has two faces;
false and sincere beware"

Positivo

Don't look for the faults in others
For such is a reflection of within
And with the tide
You'll achieve a better ride

People may come, and
People may go
Out of which
On the tide you'll row

The current may change
From smooth to roughness
And so, maybe your thoughts
Hold on, that's where love you'll find

Time and tide waits for no man
Nevertheless, you have to take that chance
That will give you substance
"look for the good in others"
So that you build on your own
Thus, without any sorrow
There will be a better tomorrow

In each of us there is goodness
Let's suppress the negativeness
And be witness to others' betterness

"A smile is a welcome;
A frown is a disapproval"

My Father's Words
Tribute to My Father.... same name

My son, be good for goodness sake
So that you can be at your happiest when you wake
These things are true my child
For you will look back, and realize how the years had flown.

In life, some of us go through a torpor,
Unknowing the reason this is for
Trust that such could be only a test
For a better and lasting tomorrow

What more can I ask?
To see you grow as I wanted you to
With hope that all would be well for you
My son, my son, I plead to you; fear no man, do no wrong
For some day, some day you will be respected and strong

Remember, my son, what I have
promised you
Have no fear; it will come true
Sometimes you may be humiliated,
resented or disliked
At other times, however, you will be praised with delight
At all times be calm, considerate, and polite

Your brother differs in many ways.
Yet, do not forsake him, not even for a day
For though you are the first and feel
 pushed aside
I know your patience and understanding would be your guide.

Now, my time has come to depart to rest

Whether it is a wish or command,
God knows best
Trust me; always keep my words in
your mind
And you would unquestionably
accredit the Divine.

"Forgiveness is a virtue; try it sometime""
"Once a man, twice a child"
"Don't swim in waters you can't see"

Published in Windows of The Soul, 1997

Our Brother and Us

Dedicated to Charmaine and Andrew

Why must we suffer from our fellow man?
Why must we weep for our brother?
'Tis not because he has done us wrong
But, because we wish he was better

Times he tries to segregate and humiliate us
Such, I know not as a child
For me, the creator made all alike
But, when I became an adult, I recognized
My brother's dislike

When will my brother ever learn?
'Tis not the harmony and a tolerant air
This diseased man has manifested within himself.
Some have concealed it with a cloak of Divinity
which is absurd to all and sundry

To him, others with a different shade of skin are in inferior kind
even though we outnumbered him many, many times
He exploits, he divides, and he controls our economic size
This, he achieves by influencing within
Or, Take arms against a sea of trouble and, by opposing, ends them
No, these trials can be conquered by tolerance, forgiveness, and most
of all consciousness.
That we are all members of the human race

An altruistic manifestation is a must,
Sometimes in the future for our brother and us.

*This poem was published in Songs of Senses
The International Library of Poetry 1999

Epitaph

I know I am not here forever
In my life I'll try to leave it better
And when I go
Remember me
For my smile
Remember me
For my tolerance
Remember me
For our friendship
Remember me
And try to forgive my failures
Remember me
May your memories of me be kind,
Remember me
For happy moments we had
Remember me
As I prevented our days to be sad
Remember me
As we enjoyed each other's company
Remember me
With each other's special memory.

The Bird

(Soliloquy as a bird)

As I stood in a tree up high
To take my sleep for the night
The lake beneath is peaceful tonight
Then, suddenly, I hear the bullfrogs croak

A school of fish breaks the surface
Whilst in the background are the crickets
Organizing a song, or discussion
The moon rises slowly in the distance
As it reflects on the surface of the water

Nocturnal creatures emerge from the forest
With intentions to seek what they can digest
As I prepare for the night's rest
With hope that I would be safe
Until the dawn breaks

My freedom is but a simple kind
That lingers on with time
Throughout the years of flying free
The time is soon approaching
To seek a mate for me

And when I do
With my brood on the way
My cherished life is near its end
Just as my parents before me
It would be the time to say: Let it be.

The Forest

Since the beginning of time
When the earth was young and blind
I and my kind have stood silently watching

Listened to the music of each dawn
Stood silent in the twilight of night
As one with the cosmos
Surrounded by the peace of forest ways

Watched seasons unfold
In those flowers of time
which from a tiny bud grew
and blossomed, and passed

Surrounded by creatures both day and night
that gave their dance of life as they multiplied
with time passing by.

I, and my kind, have watched men
Who came and went, the birth of nations
The rise and fall of man
Their happiness and their sorrow

I have protected birds to bees in my canopy
I give balance to your ecology
and medicine for everybody.
Yet, the said mankind destroys me
by using his saw daily

Ignoring the ravages of time
I and my kind
Like man, must stand and wait
For the miracle of a new dawn
"Time brings in changes"

My Mind

My mind is in a cave
Where I can hide
Lots of secrets with me
Side by side

In my mind
I can swear
However from my mouth
I would not dare

In my mind
There is a plan
For you and me
I would write in the sand

And when I am asleep
My mind is at its peak
With memories of you
That I can speak

Oh, how I love my mind
It's my only treasure
No one can take
Thank God it's with me
Asleep or Awake Forever

This gift I have
It is also with you
Our minds are our own
Not to give nor on loan

My Dream

I dream of a world where man
knows how to take care of himself
Where he will share such knowledge with others
and where there will be peace everywhere

I dream of a world where man acknowledges everyone was created equal
Where none shall conceive they are better
Where economic achievement makes no difference

I dream of a world of hope
of happiness and of peace
Where none would kill or hurt another
for material prosperity

To sit by the stream to watch its waters flow
To listen to birds chirping brightly
To see butterflies fluttering
from flower to flower
Such is the stuff of My Dream

I dream of a world where man shall share laughter and pain, tears and smiles
For we are all vulnerable to mother's law
When illness comes to our door

In the dark eastern sky, we see stars
Such is signpost led us to be free
Silence is queen over the calm, still sea
Night has a mystery

And such is the mystery of the heart
that is longing to be free
My dream will create such a borough
In which freedom will be possible tomorrow.

Your Hand

Lord, givest thou thy hand
The rivers and seas are deep and wide.
The pit is not as shallow as I thought,
Therefore, forget me not
Lord, please givest thou thy hand

The mountain is exceedingly high
I need your strength by my side
The road is long with much dismay,
For on my way I may go astray,
Therefore, I pray
Lord, givest thou thy hand

Your comfort, love, and assurance
Are the guardians of reliance
No one can go through this life
Without you by their side
Therefore, Lord, givest thou thy hand

Our forefathers held your hand passing
Through the needle's eye
With such, they slip, not slide
Having such confidence,
I shall maintain my obedience,
Therefore, Lord, givest thou thy hand

I thank you, Lord
For you choosing me this day
To follow you all the way.
My adversities and success
Were written for me
I plea, Lord, please givest thou thy hand.

My Secret Place

My secret place is there to hide,
A place where I have often cried
A place where no one judges you
And criticisms are few
A peaceful atmosphere
A hiding place to shed a little
Laughter or tears

This secret place is with all of us
We go there frequently to meditate
So as to apply what we call intricate
A place to relive what was great
In this place laughter can fill the air
Above all, you don't care

This place no one can share
It is safe and secure
No anxiety to endure
As it is with mine
This wonderful place you'll find
Is hidden in the recesses of your mind
For it's yours and yours alone.

Love

As I walk through the corridors of time
I found that love has its sublime
The ascetic of its transcendence
Gives a glance of what would be
A sense of spiritual love for you and me

Such love will last forever
And can grow and never falter
Because this love is given by our maker
An emotion we can impart to another
With sensitivity and reciprocality

This love is based on internal and external consideration
A love that others can see
It had to be

There is, however, another love, its twin
It can disguise itself for its objective
An objective of self-gratification
It is passionate with tolerance
For its purpose is a physical kind
When achieved, its interest declines

Diotima made it clear
Love from above can be dear
And can be physical and spiritual
Such linkage is approved from above
What God has joined together,
No man can put asunder

As Diotima said "This love is the
Foundation that leads to absolute
And unadulterated beauty
of love itself"

Rosalie

Rosalie, a fair rose with such a sweet name
A person whom we found without blame
I reminisce the days gone by
Of such a charming lady by my side
In sorrow or joy she was there
Which strengthened me, and let me be without fear
Oh, Rosalie, your time was best spent
Caring for us, even if it caused inconvenience
You showed no indicator for gain for oneself
Rosalie, though you are not with us anymore
We miss your antiphony
For when it's heard from the living
You are reconstructed within
Rosalie, how sweet a name
A person whom we found without blame
May the angles take care of you
And bless you among the few
Tis my grandmother I speak of
Who had given us the precious gift
Of care and unending love, you fair rose.
The truth is beneath the surface
The greatness gift is Love

Published in Dream of Everyday, 1997, by The Poetry Guild

Middle Passage

He is a man who walks in quiet,
carefully avoiding streams of endless verbosity
Wrapped firmly in his convictions,
not trusting empty paragraphs of promises
Believing only in the unity of his people,
one people from our homeland.
We were taken away to this foreign land.
We were led astray, forced to live as servants and slaves.
Living in bondage, compelled to obey.
This is Our Past, not a gift but a curse.
We've lived through abuse, degradation, and worse.
Over the years wehave won our fight;
to be treated equal is our birthright, cultivating the world.
We've made this race our own.
Making this foreign land our new home.
Together we've overcome the chains that held us down.
Together we must stop the slavery of now:
IGNORANCE, DRUGS, CRIME, AND ILLITERACY
Only we can stop these self-seeking acts of conspiracy.
Only as one will we succeed to be in our new homeland TOTALLY FREE
A smile is a welcome
A frown is disapproval

Adverse Times

Tough times come to everyone
Young and old, weak and strong
Sad times happen now and again
Just as sunny days are followed by
days of rain

Tears maybe many
Debts can be mountain
And though your smile may fade today
Be certain you'll see victory another day

With every success
There lies some stress
Before every victory
There is a chance of failure

Tough times never last
But tough people always do
Rough times come and go
As tough people see it through

So, when adverse comes your way
Hold on, for you will be happy one day
You were born a fighter
Be assured, someday, things will be better.

Adversities shows us where
lies our success

Knowledge

What I know, you can know
For I'm not here forever
So take what I know and grow
I have learned many things
In this life journey
Through others experiences
Through my own experiences
Most of all
I have learned that knowledge
of life should be shared
For each of us has something to give
So what I know you can know
Take the time, take my wheel
Don't reinvent, just make it better for you
This knowledge will open avenues for you
Once you got it pass it on
Allowing avenues to open for others
What you know others should know
What I know you can know.

- Pass on knowledge; it's a good deed –

Open Thy Self

Open thy self to me
Hide not your inner self
For I wish to know your true self
Your outer self has captured me
Now I must know your inner self
For in time your true inner self will emerge
And, I may or may not be disappointed
So, open to me thy inner self before it's too late
Does time really bring about a change in a person?
Or is it the true inner self that comes out in time.
Open thy self to me
Hide not your inner self.

Siblings

Oh sisters, Oh brothers
Why have you changed towards me?
As children we played, we teased, we cared for each other
We laugh, we cried, we had fun and loved each other
So why my sisters, why my brothers
Have you changed towards me?
We shared secrets
We had good times and bad times
But most of all we had fun
We loved each other, we had each other
So why my sisters, why my brothers, have you changed towards me
Why do you allow my thinking to change your love of me?
Why can't you continue to love me, the way we were as children.
Now we are grown we think differently
But that should not stop our love
Now we are grown we can still laugh and cry together
I can't think like you nor can you think like me
But we can still love each other and still have fun.
The paths we took in life are different
But that should not stop our love for each other.
Agree to disagree is a form of caring. And as adults
We should still care and love each other even
If we don't think alike, we should still have fun
and keep the bond
So my sisters and my brothers, think of our lives
Now that we are old and grey our love should
Be stronger today

CPSIA information can be obtained
at www.ICGtesting.com
Printed in the USA
LVHW071357060922
727702LV00011B/340